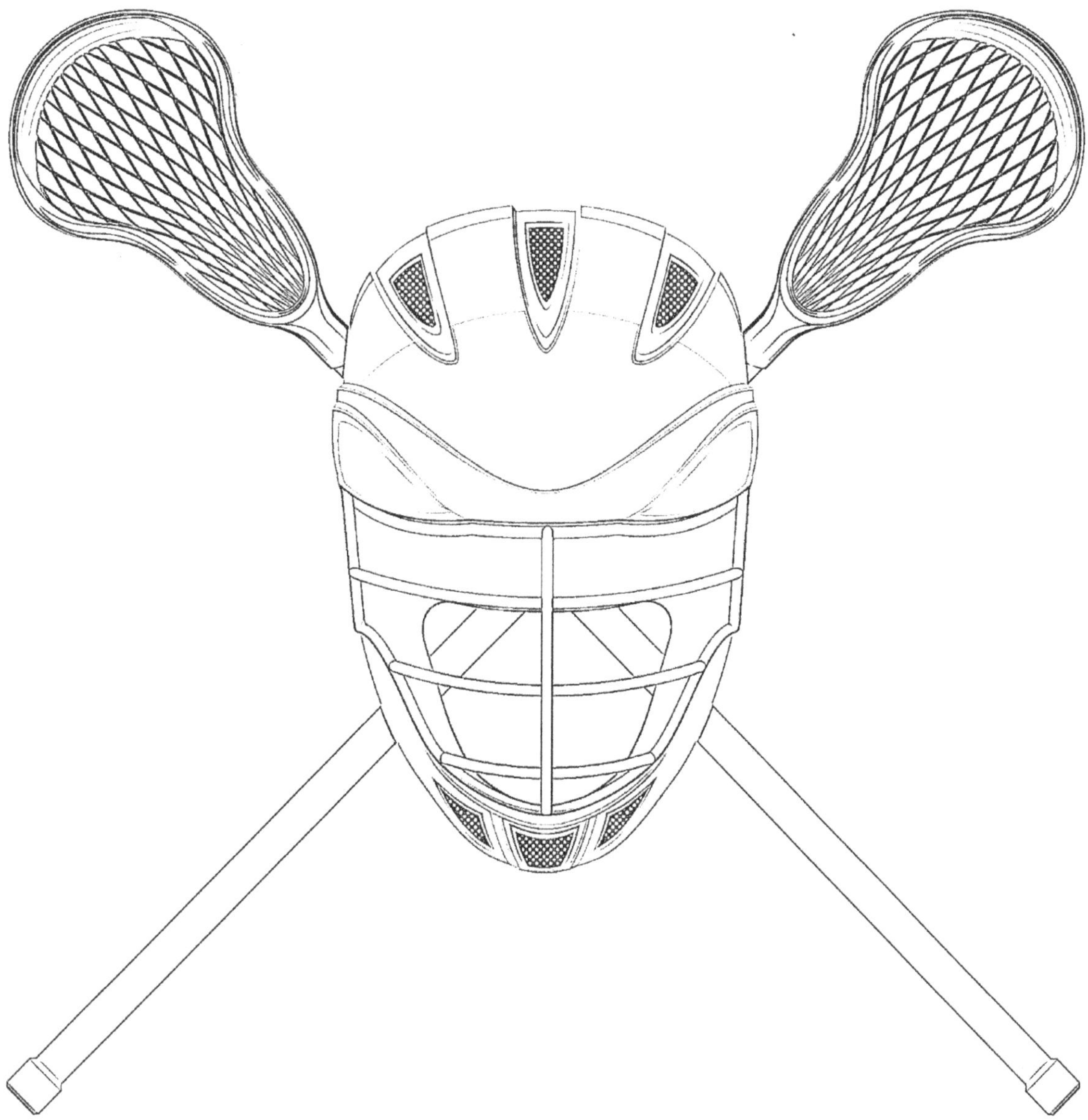

LACROSSE

LacrossE

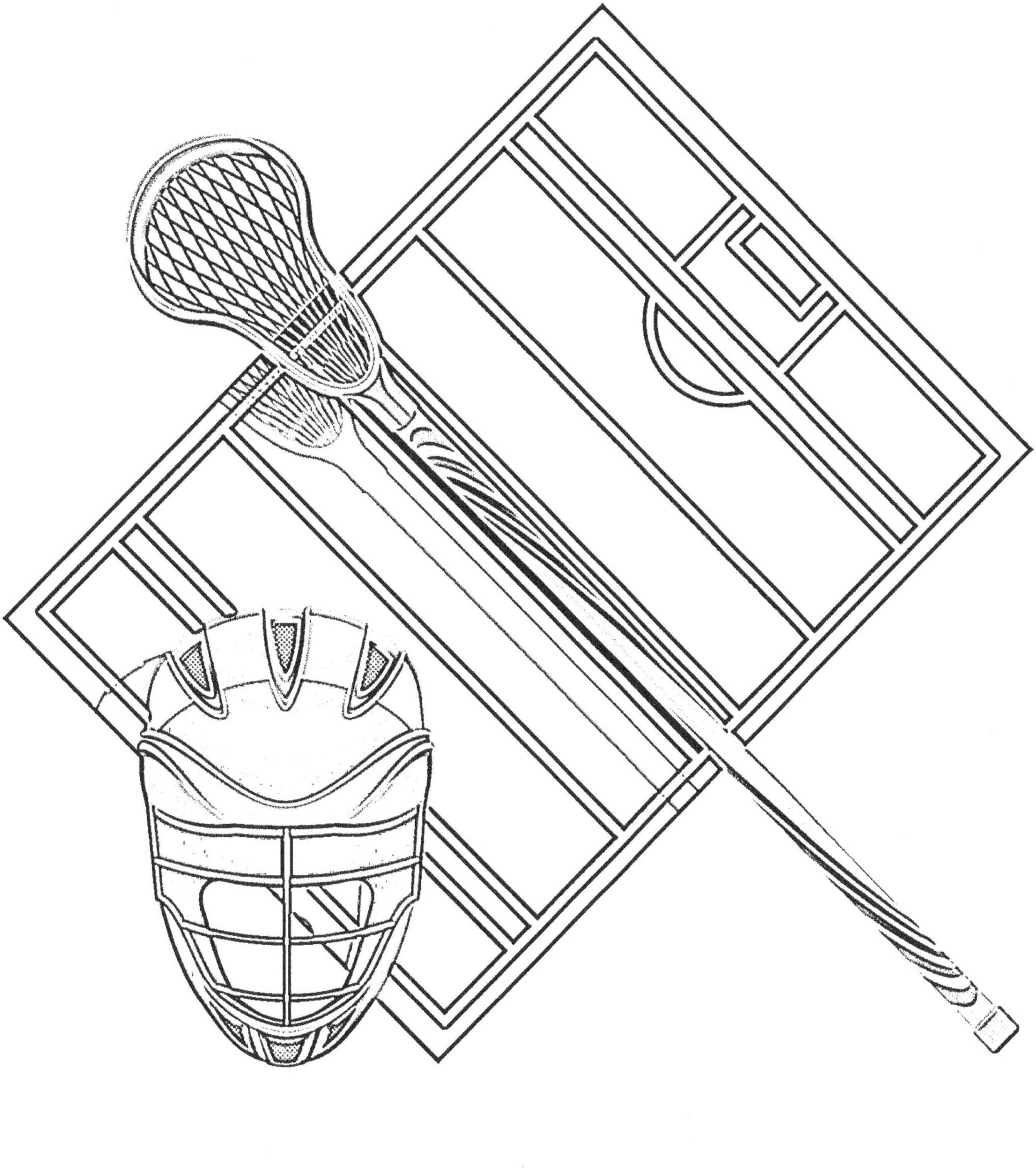

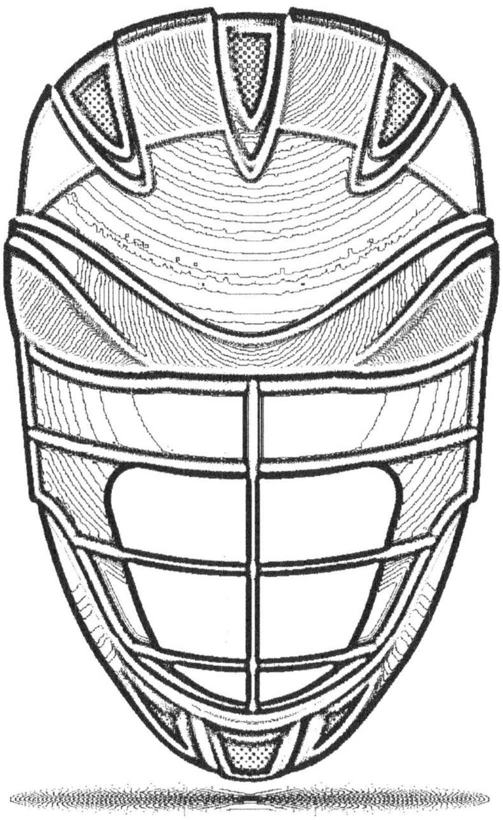
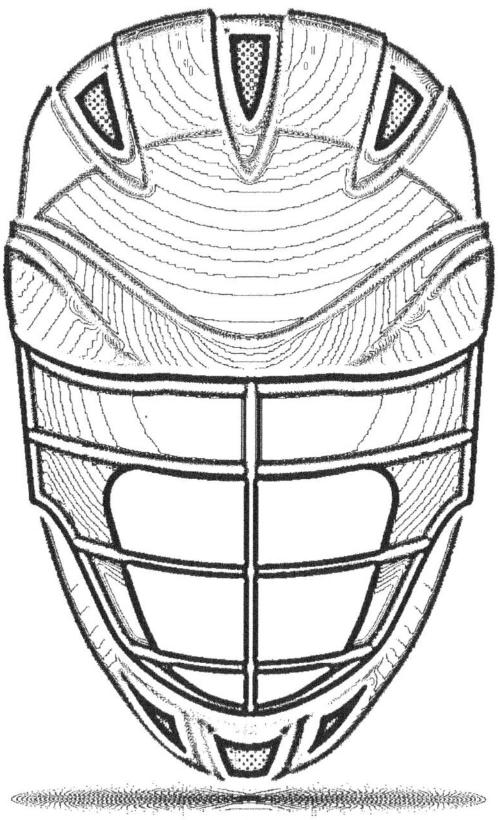
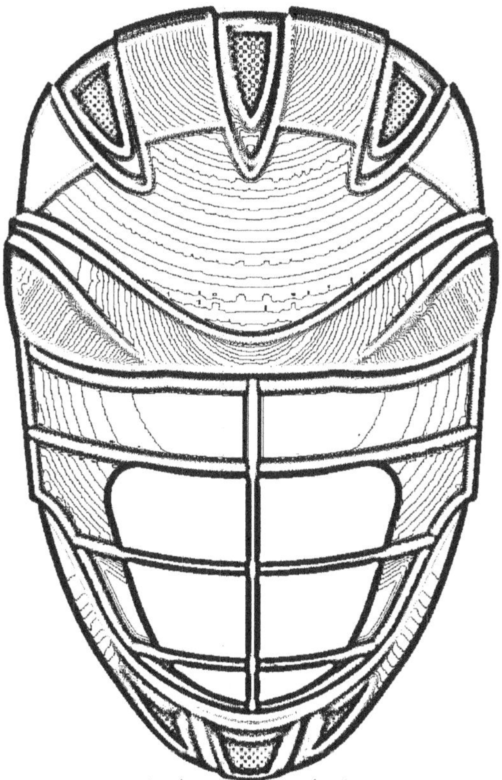
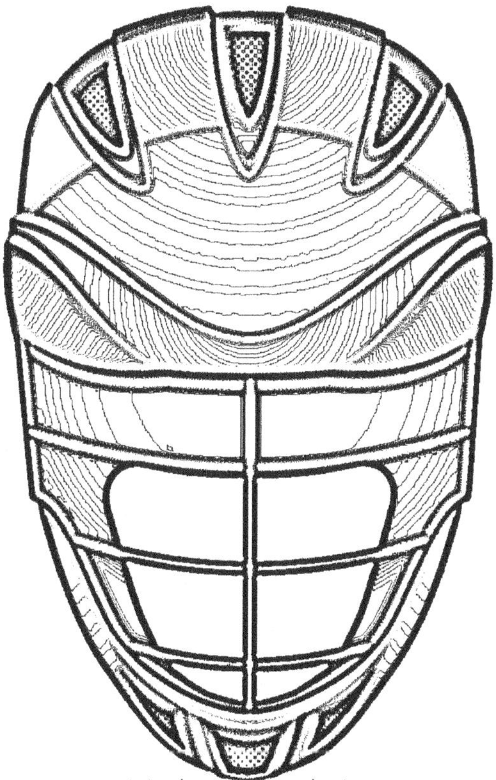

1

12:31
07:69
TICKET
TICKET
1

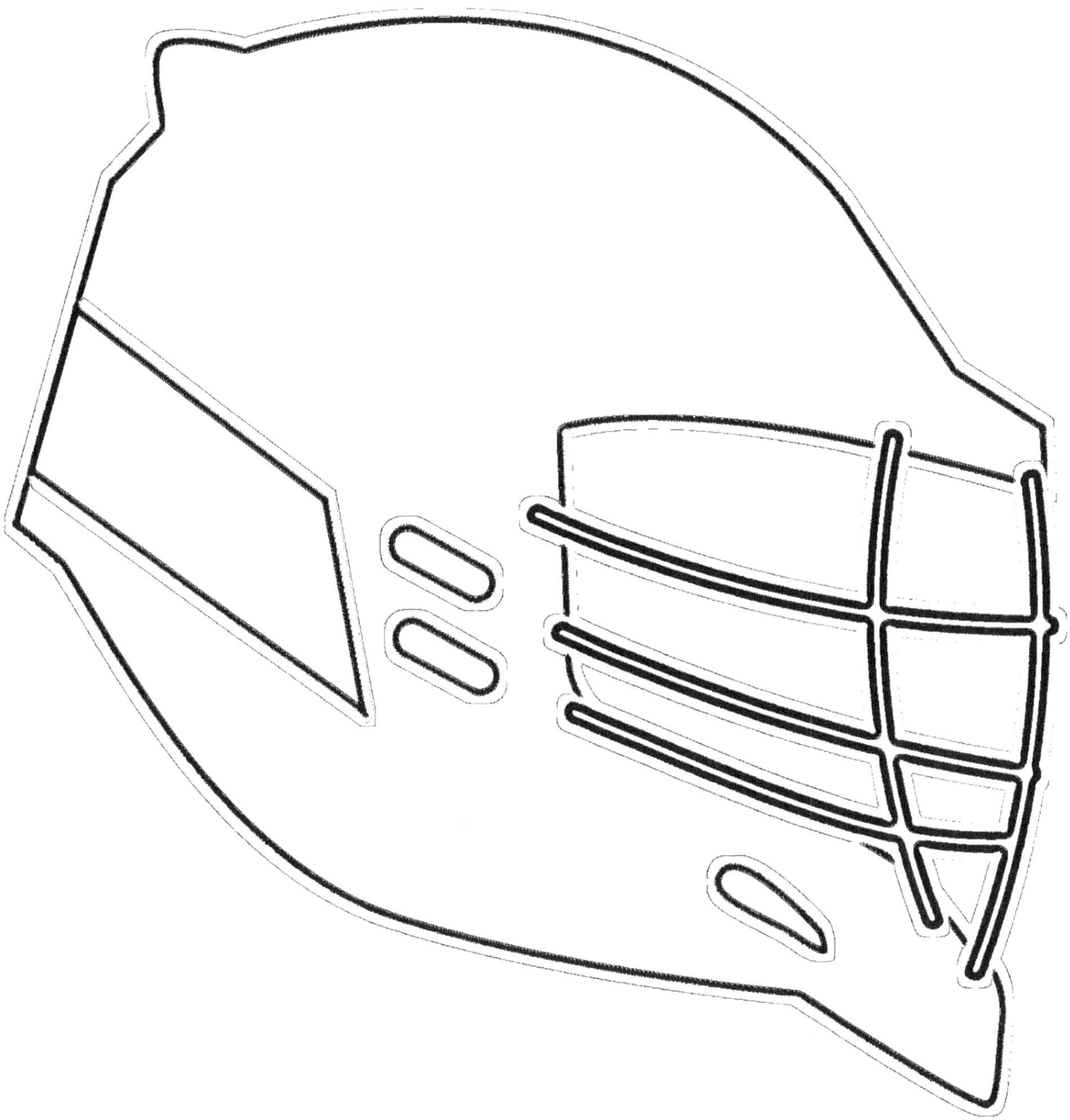

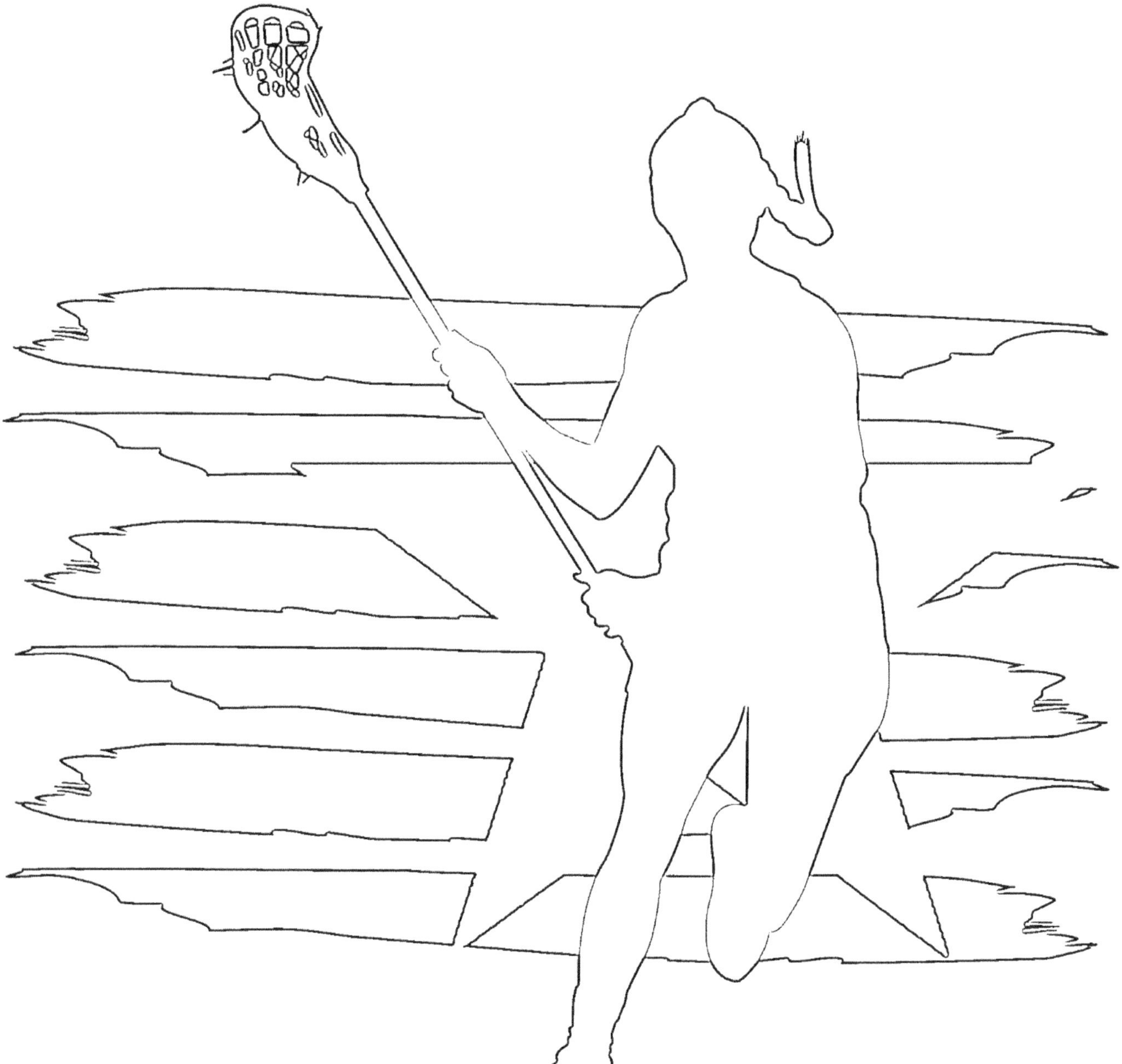

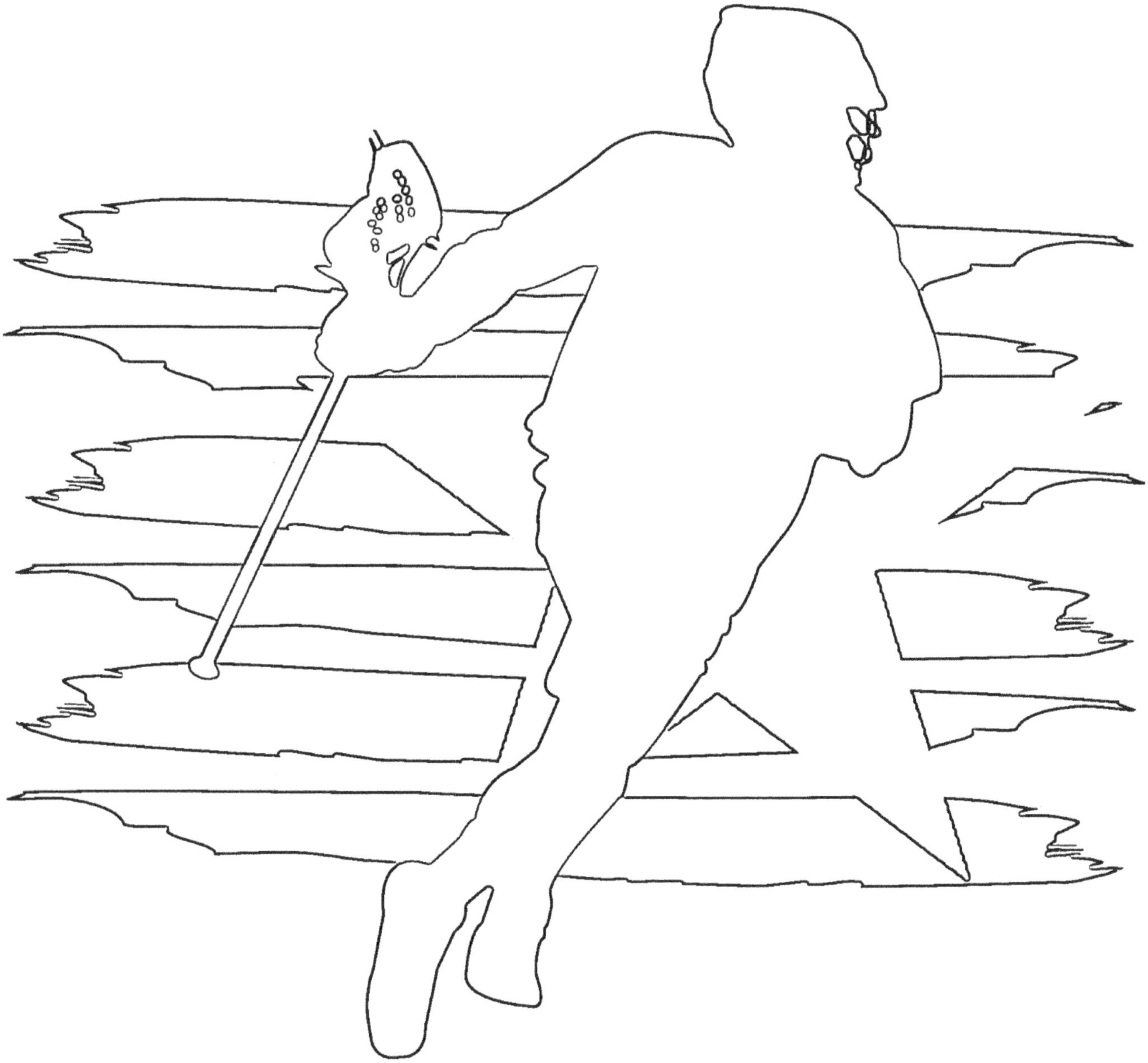

Lacrosse

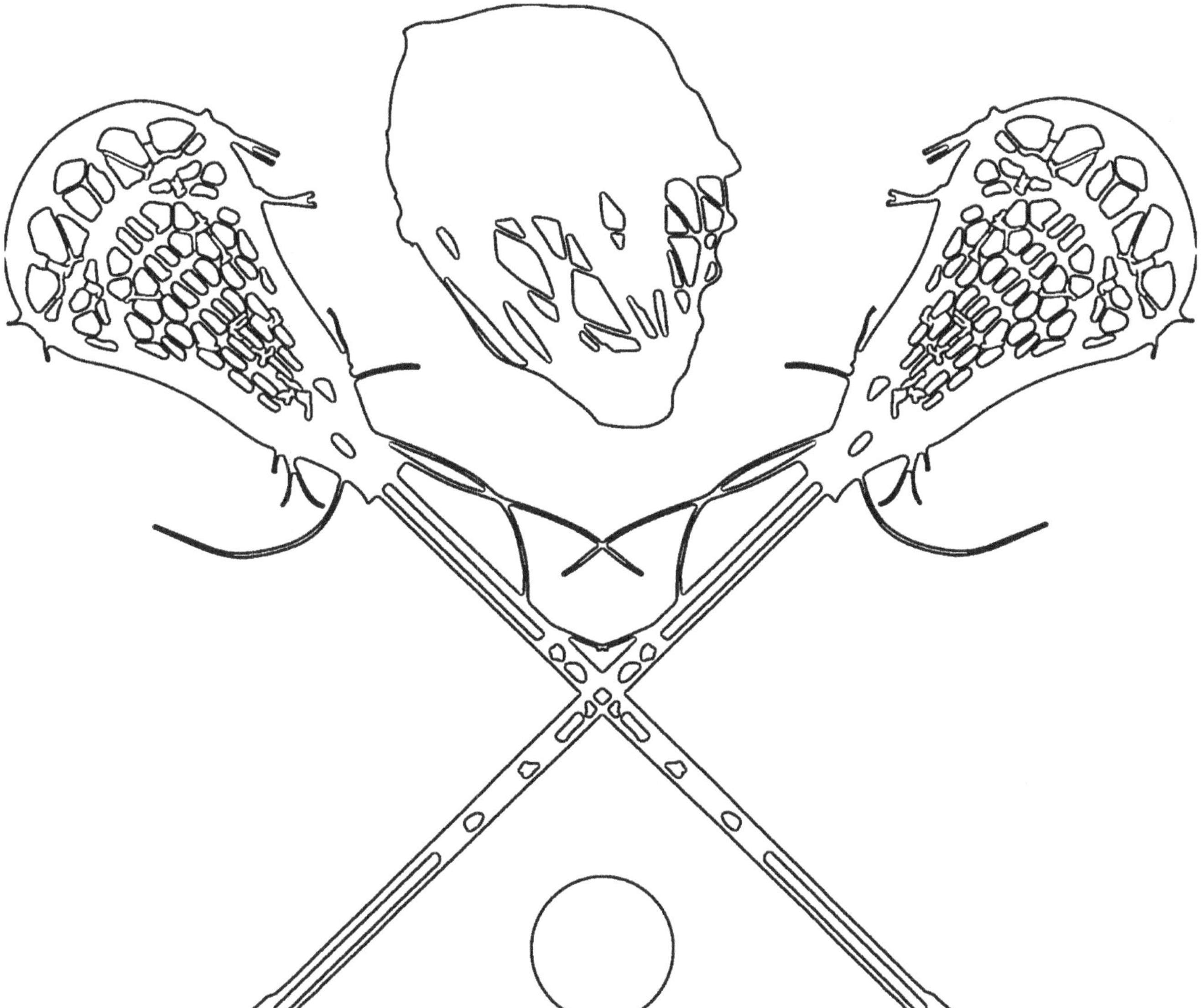

LACROSSE

Lacrosse
Lacrosse

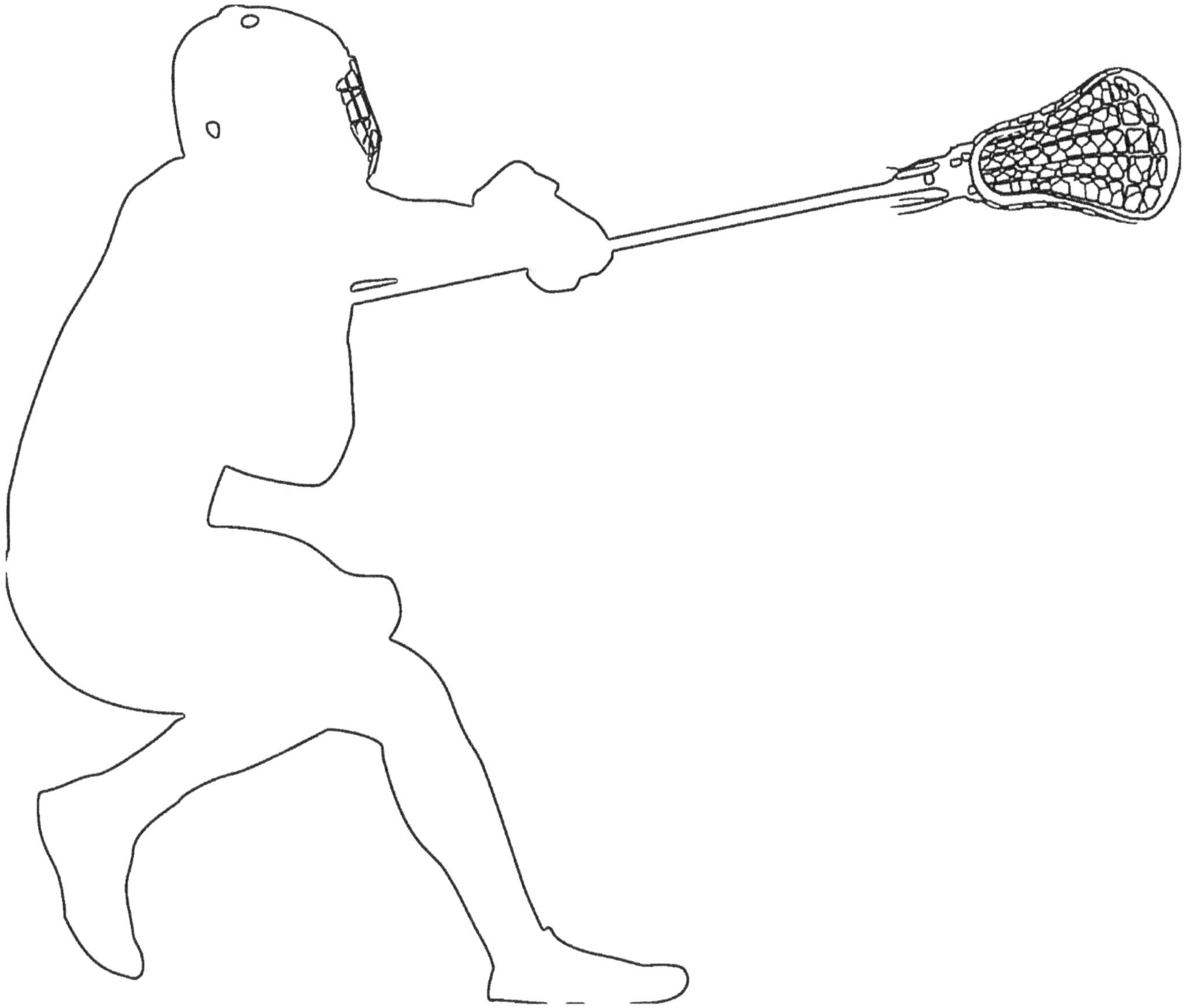

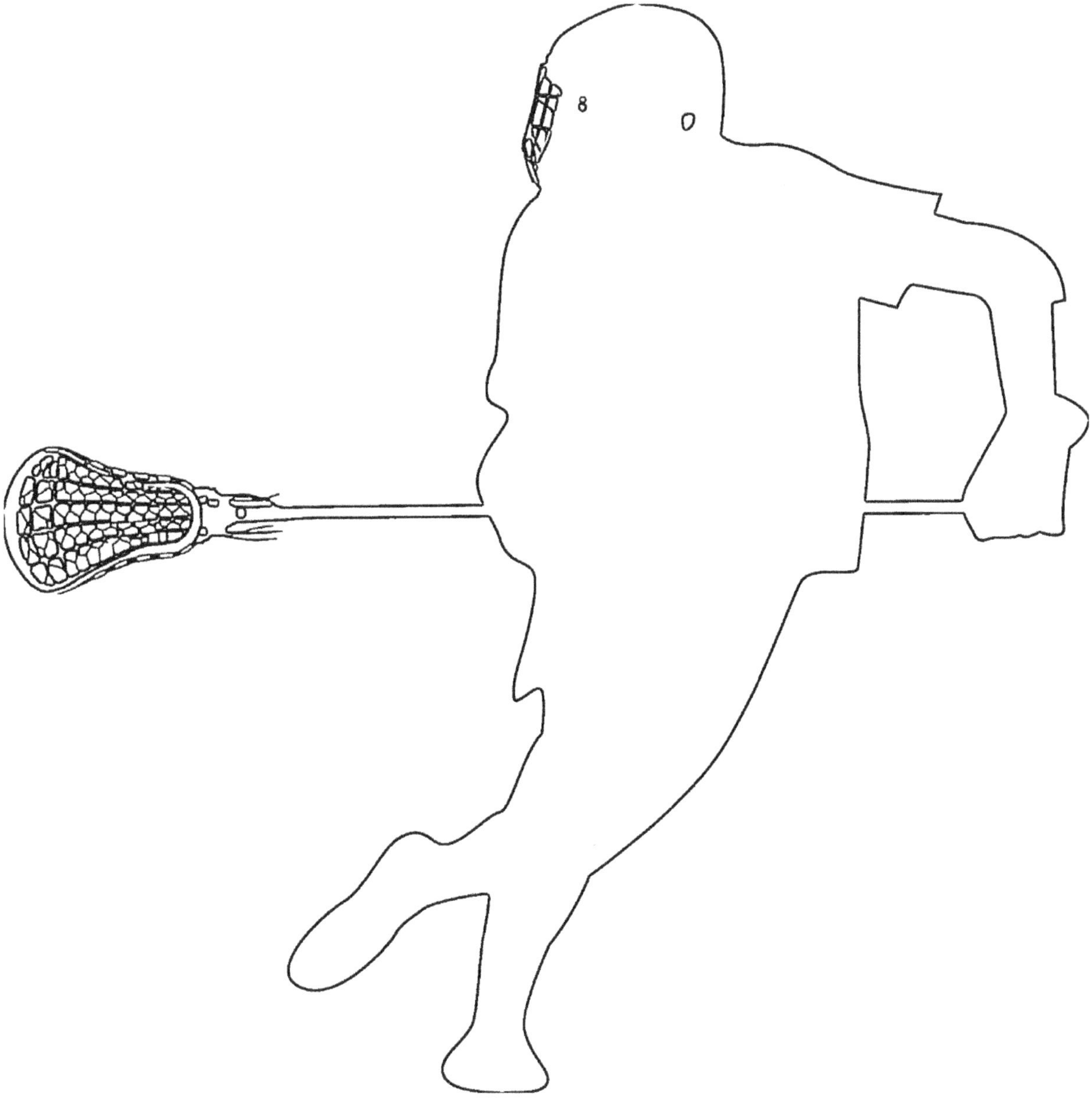

LOVE ME
LOVE
LACROSSE

Made in the USA
Coppell, TX
23 August 2021

60950869R00031